THE TERM PAPER
Step by Step

GILBERT KAHN is a graduate of Rider College who holds B.S., M.A. and Ed.D. degrees from New York University. During his 32-year career he has taught in high schools, colleges, and adult schools. He is now Chairman of the Business Department of East Side High School in Newark, New Jersey, and in 1963 was the recipient of the Princeton University Distinguished Secondary School Teaching Prize.

Dr. Kahn is co-author of eight texts in the business field and the author of numerous professional articles. He and his wife, who live in Verona, New Jersey, have two grown sons.

DONALD J. D. MULKERNE received his B.S. and Ed.M. degrees from Boston University and his Ed.D. from Columbia University. He has a wide teaching experience including posts at Russell Sage College, College of St. Rose, Catholic University of America, Columbia University, and his present position as Professor and Chairman of the Department of Office Administration at the State University of New York at Albany.

Dr. Mulkerne is the author of numerous texts and articles for professional journals. He and his wife and their seven children live in Delmar, New York.

THE TERM PAPER
Step by Step

GILBERT KAHN, Ed.D.
East Side High School
Newark, New Jersey

DONALD J. D. MULKERNE, Ed. D.
State University of New York
at Albany

DOUBLEDAY & COMPANY, INC.
GARDEN CITY, NEW YORK

TABLE OF CONTENTS

THE TERM PAPER
Step by Step

Chapter I

INTRODUCTION

The Purpose of This Manual

This book is designed to help you write your term paper—indeed any research paper for which you must plan carefully to find, organize, and present information from a number of sources—whether this paper is your first or your twentieth.

It is a basic source of reference which will:

Help you choose a subject

Show you how to get the most out of library resources

Explain the purpose of the bibliography and footnotes as well as the mechanics of presenting them

Suggest note-taking techniques

Guide you in developing an outline

Assist you in writing a paper from your outline so it will be prepared in acceptable style

Show you how to set up simple tables

Provide you with step-by-step procedures for typing the final copy from your draft in the proper form

Include a finished term paper to illustrate the various procedures covered in this manual

Why Term Papers?

Why do college students have to prepare term papers? Skills in English usage and experience in expressing ideas on paper in a readable and interesting manner can be acquired by writing original expository themes. The preparation of a research paper, however, offers further challenges to you. It demands that you display your qualifications to be called an "educated person" by demonstrating the ability to gather, interpret, and report on facts and ideas impartially, honestly, and clearly.

Preparing a term paper will:

Give you experience in locating information quickly and choosing among available sources as well as acquainting you with the library resources from which information can be drawn

Give you a broad and thorough grasp of the subject area on which you write

Teach you selectivity, for you will do much more reading than writing for your paper and you must not only choose from your reading what should be included in your paper, but judge the relative importance of that information to your context

And, of course, develop your writing skills and vocabulary so you can communicate more effectively.

WHAT THE TERM PAPER IS NOT

The term paper is not a thesis or a dissertation. These two graduate papers go much more deeply into a particular subject and require a great deal of time, effort, research, and extensive bibliography. In many cases, statistical interpretations are made. The term paper is less formal, shorter, shows evidence of some reading background, contains a usually concise bibliography, and does not often make use of statistical procedures.

However, the term paper is not a popular novel. It should keep to facts, treat *pro* and *con* data fairly, and present its evidence in a scholarly manner, while being interesting to read.

Neither is a term paper a mere listing of what several sources have to say about its topic. This kind of writing is lifeless, boring, and adds nothing to the knowledge already available on the subject. A worth-while paper has form, its own introduction and conclusions.

Finally, a term paper is not:

A pseudoscholarly collection or barrage of footnotes which serve only to require the reader to break his line of thought by darting his eyes back and forth from context to footnote.

A summary of one book or of one person. Rather the term paper represents an orchestra of information by making use of many different sources.

A carelessly written composition riddled with errors of grammar, logic, and mechanics.

An attempt at original research of the laboratory-experimentation type commonly employed in doctoral dissertations.

WHAT THE TERM PAPER IS

Your term paper should be an unbiased account of a topic documented with pertinent and valid information in support of whatever statements you make.

Your paper may be of the argumentative or of the storytelling type. The argumentative paper attempts to prove that something is right or wrong, good or bad, desirable or undesirable, while the storytelling type surveys a subject by drawing upon pertinent references bearing upon a particular point, and then is written about the highlights of what has been read, without attempting to prove or disprove anything. The sample paper illustrated at the end of this manual is of the storytelling type.

Documentation—the use of quotations—is a distinguishing feature of term papers. Each quotation must carry a footnote which identifies its source since it is important in this type of paper to know who said what. These quotations must be carefully selected and used only when really necessary to bring out a point you are trying to make. Too many quotations make for a choppy paper, and your instructor will note that he is reading what a lot of other people think rather than what you think as illustrated by your choice of quotations. Failure to identify quoted matter and passing it off as one's own is *dishonest* and may well result in a failing mark.

The term paper, while its content is drawn from numerous sources, has the style of a well-written composition. Simply expressed, your paper will contain a short statement of its purpose, followed by your evidence presented in a logical manner and arranged for smooth reading. The paper will be completed with a few appropriate remarks which summarize the highlights of your research. Any conclusions you draw must be based upon your evidence.

Furthermore, the language of the paper will be related to its purpose. Are you trying to persuade, explain, relate, or entertain? Once you have decided this, you will know the degree of formality your paper should assume and the kind of vocabulary you should use. (Borrowing "twenty dollar words" without fully understanding their meaning may result in the wrong choices.) Avoid trying to lengthen your paper by adding extra words just to reach a minimum set by your instructor. Conciseness, rather than wordiness, and simplicity, rather than floweriness, should be your stylistic goals.

Finally, the term paper reflects you and the quality of your thinking. It should be factual and at the same time fair, including all evidence you find in your readings even though some of it may weaken your original position about your subject. Remember that progress is also made by discovering that what you once thought to be true is in fact false. What would you think of a pharmaceutical firm that put a drug on the market, guaranteed it to cure the common cold but failed to inform the public that severe headaches would result from its use? It is just as dishonest to mislead your reader by failing to include evidence contrary to your viewpoint and in so doing commit a serious error of omission. Such "slanting" is not likely to go unnoticed.

The most difficult job in writing is to get started. Begin where it is easiest for you: sit down and write all you now know about your subject—if you have one. If you have yet to select a subject, turn to Chapter II.

How Is This Book to Be Used?

This manual provides key ideas to show you—as closely as any book can—exactly how to go about writing your paper. These key ideas are expressed in short simple sentences, each of which is numbered consecutively. As you will see, these numbers have been noted on the sample term paper at the end of the book, so you may easily look up the explanation or the reason for the use of a particular form.

CHAPTER II

CHOOSING AND LIMITING THE SUBJECT

Choosing a subject is deceptively difficult and should not be treated lightly. While it may seem to require less physical effort than the other parts of preparing a paper, deciding on an appropriate subject and limiting it to a degree where you can give it the attention it needs will in the long run result in a completed paper of which you can be proud. Don't jump into choosing a topic. Selecting a topic impulsively or intuitively may cause you to regret your haste, for your paper may later bog down to a discouraging halt. Reflect upon each of the following suggestions, for they will help you get off to a good start.

1. Understand your assignment.

> Listen to your instructor as he describes your term paper assignment. Understand its purpose, the length of the paper, the due date, the limits within which you must confine your subject, the type of paper you are to prepare—argumentative or storytelling. Keep your instructor's comments on file and refer to them frequently.

2. Your subject may be assigned, you may choose your own, or you may choose a subject within a certain area defined by your instructor.

> If your instructor assigns you a subject, your task is simplified because you are now ready to make your plans for collecting the data. If you must choose your own subject, consider items 3 through 16. If your subject must be

confined within a certain area, such as English, History, or Geology, examine book and periodical indexes for ideas. Read Chapter III of this manual and then if you have questions, consult with your college or local librarian.

3. Think about your assignment and if your instructor has invited discussion, go to him with your ideas.

    Develop a tentative plan of attack by listing reference books, indexes, periodicals, and other aids which may be of assistance to you. If term papers are on file for student examination, read several for your paper. Make a list of questions to ask your instructor. You are now ready for your initial interview with him.

4. The title of your subject may be in the form of a question or a positive statement.

    Subjects for term papers expressed in question form:
    Of What Value Are Term Papers to College Students?
    What Are the Requisites for Success in Business?
    What Can Be Done to Help Reduce Juvenile Delinquency?
    What Compelled Booth to Kill Lincoln?
    Subjects for term papers expressed as positive statements:
    The Influence of Unions on the Safety of Workers
    Color and Lighting for Office Illumination
    A Suggested Plan for Utilizing Television as a Learning Aid
    Booth and His Motives for Killing Lincoln

5. Select a subject in line with the basic purposes of your course.

    If you are completing a term paper for an English course, consider the advisability of writing about a subject in the English area. Determine the purpose of your term paper. Consider the reason that motivated your instructor to request such an assignment from you. As a result of writing your paper, are you supposed to be a better writer, a better thinker, a better researcher, or better informed about your subject? Knowing the reason for your assignment will help you write a paper in keeping with the requirements of your course.

6. Select a subject in which you have a strong interest, curiosity, experience, or competency.

> When interest and curiosity are present, your term paper becomes a delightful experience rather than a chore. Prior experience and competency in your subject reduce the danger of making unwise statements in your paper or failing to report the basic facts.

7. Select a subject in which information is readily available.

> The subject should not be so new that information is difficult to obtain. Generally speaking, your school library or the local library should be well equipped, so that you can do all your reading in the local area. Consult your librarian and ask her opinion about the availability of data on your chosen subject. Choose a subject in which adequate and reliable information is available.
>
> Examples of subjects having limited or unreliable data:
> Aircraft Stations in Outer Space
> U.S.A.—A.D. 3000
> The Inside Story of Security Measures Taken at Cape Canaveral
> Booth's Private Conversations with His Conspirators
> The Secret Thoughts of John Wilkes Booth
> The Genealogy of the Conspirators of Lincoln

8. Select a subject with your audience in mind.

> Consider that another human being will read your paper. If you know the viewpoint and the interest level of your instructor about your chosen subject, your paper will be more to the point and more interesting for him to read. If you know how informed your reader already is about your topic, it will be to your advantage to write a paper that goes beyond his present range of knowledge. He should learn something by reading your paper.

9. Select a subject important enough to warrant your attention, and if possible, one that correlates with other courses you are taking. In so doing you will then work with information that will help you improve in history or whatever.

> Choose a subject that is intellectually respectable, offers

practical value, and is capable of being developed fully into a thesis or a dissertation at some future time.

Examples of subjects lacking intellectual respectability or practical value:

Penguins of the South Pole (for a non-zoologist and a paper which has a travelogue flavor)

Fun at a Fair

The Manufacture of Christmas Candles

The Pizza Pie

10. Select a subject that can be researched within the time limits set by your instructor.

Determine how much time you have to complete your paper. Set deadlines for each phase of your research and writing task. Don't take on too ambitious a topic. Choose a broad subject area and then limit it.

Examples of subjects too ambitious for term papers:

Lincoln: the Full Story of the Assassination and Trial

The Rise and Fall of the Roman Empire

The Conquests of Napoleon

The World's Great Musicians

U.S. Presidents

The above topics might be used if they cover a smaller area:

Lincoln—the Last Year of His Life

The Rise of the Roman Empire

Napoleon Wins a Battle

American Composers of Jazz in the 1920s

U.S. Presidents of the Twentieth Century

11. Select a subject that is not too narrow.

Examples of subjects that are too narrow:

Lamprey Damage in Lake Huron for August 1959

Diseases of Fleas

High School Economics for First-semester Seniors in Alaska

Lincoln—His Service as a Postmaster

12. Select a subject that does not involve technical information beyond your comprehension.

Examples of subjects that might be too technical in nature:
The Thermonuclear Bomb Ingredients
Drugs for Arthritis
Xerography—How It Works
Flights of Trajectories and Their Geometric Patterns

13. Select a subject suitable for student investigation and in good taste. A sensational subject appears more often to be a childish choice rather than a clever one. Someone is going to read your paper—make his time worth while.

Examples of subjects not in good taste:
The Heroic Qualities of Dillinger
The Pleasures of Brutality
Sensational Incidences of Debauchery among the Romans

14. Select a subject that is not too neutral.

Examples of subjects too neutral:
Insurance Mortality Tables
Filing Cases
Advantages of Electricity over Gaslight

15. Select a subject that is clear.

Examples of subjects that may not be clear:
Quakers and Friends
Running for the Office
Banks

16. Select a subject that does not have a universal acceptance.

Examples of subjects that have universal acceptance:
Child Welfare Laws in the U.S.—Are They Desirable?
AA—Does It Serve a Useful Purpose?
Did John Wilkes Booth Kill Lincoln?

Chapter III

USING THE LIBRARY

The library is an educational tool. To get the greatest benefit from it, you must use it wisely. When you consider how often you will need the services of the library, you can appreciate the value of becoming skilled in library procedure. The benefits to be derived from wise use of the library facilities are numerous, but two override all others: pertinent references are easily located and time is saved when you "know your way around" in the library.

17. Most libraries prepare a set of instructions on how to use the facilities most effectively. Obtain a copy and study it.

18. Material found in the library usually is of three types:
    general information
    reference materials
    periodicals

19. The library usually has a reference room.
    The reference room contains encyclopedias, magazines, newspapers, and dictionaries of various types. Materials in this room are not available for overnight use.

20. Become familiar with the various collections in the library and understand how they can be used.

21. Librarians are available to answer intelligent questions. Understand clearly the nature of your problem before you approach them for help.

22. Use 3- by 5-inch white lined cards to record the references on your subject.

23. Do some preliminary research to be sure you can locate information easily on your chosen subject. Proceed as follows:

> Develop a preliminary bibliography (using 3 by 5 cards), listing references bearing on your subject. One of the following references will serve to give you an overview of your subject as a basis for further development:
> Columbia Encyclopedia
> Compton's Pictured Encyclopedia
> Encyclopedia Americana
> Encyclopaedia Britannica
> Encyclopedia of Educational Research
> Encyclopedia of the Social Sciences
> New International Year Book from 1907
> The New International Illustrated Encyclopedia
> World Book Encyclopedia

24. Other sources in the library that will help you locate information include the following references:

> card catalog, periodical indexes, vertical files, or all three
> *See Nos. 27 and 34* for examples of the card catalog and periodical indexes. Vertical files are file cases in which are stored various and sundry matter such as booklets and catalogs received by the library. Consult the *Vertical File Index* listing such material from 1935.

25. The card catalog generally lists only books, although some libraries list periodicals which are bound. The catalog is made up of 3- by 5-inch unlined white cards either in type or print listing all books, reference books, and other contents of the library.

See No. 27.

26. The card catalog lists each book three ways:

> author, title, and subject.
> *See No. 27.*

27. The card catalog includes typed cards prepared by the local
    library.

Call or Classification No. —— 921   Bishop, James Alonzo
Autnor ——————————— L   The day Lincoln was shot. With illus.
Title ————————————   selected and arr. by Stefan Lorant.   New York,
Copyright date ———————   Harper c1955
                                    308p. illus.
    Autnor Card   Includes bibliography.

Title Card

921   The day Lincoln was shot.   c1955
L   Bishop, James Alonzo

Subject Card

921   Lincoln, Abraham,   pres. U.S. Assassins-
L   tion
       Bishop, James Alonzo
           The day Lincoln was shot. With illus.
       selected and arr. by Stefan Lorant.   New York,
       Harper c1955
           308p. illus.
           Includes bibliography.

28. The card catalog also has printed cards obtained from the Library of Congress. These cards provide the same general information as the local library cards shown in No. 27.

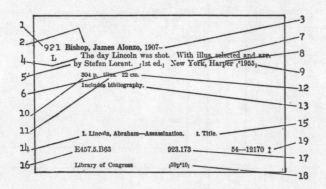

1 Call or Classification No.
2 Author
3 Date of birth of author
4 Title of book
5 Name of illustrator
6 Edition
7 Place of publication
8 Publisher
9 Copyright date
10 No. of pages in book

11 Book is illustrated
12 Size of type
13 Book has bibliography
14 Information for librarian
15 Information for librarian
16 Library of Congress Catalog no.
17 Dewey Decimal Classification no.
18 Library of Congress information
19 Card order no.

29. If several books are listed for the same author and have the same title, examine the most recent one first, as it is assumed to be the most nearly correct and up to date in its treatment of the subject matter.

30. If references are not listed under your subject title, you may be referred by "See" and "See also" cards to similar topics.

"See" Card

Manslaughter   see

Assassination
Homicide
Murder

"See also" Card

Assassination   see also

Anarchism and anarchists
Murder
Regicides
Terrorism

31. All books have author, subject, and title cards. For some books, such as a collection of poems or biographies, another type of card may be prepared, known as an analytic card. This card serves to call your attention to a small portion of another book which carries information on your subject.

> For example, if you wished to write a term paper on the assassination of Abraham Lincoln, you might note the following reference on an analytic card if you were to check the card catalog under Lincoln:

```
Analytic card              920      Lincoln, Abraham,        pres. U.S.
                            B
Call or Classification            Bradford, Gamaliel
     number                       (In his Portraits and personalities.)
Author
Copyright date                    [c1933]       p. 40-56
Clue as to where to
   look for information
   on Lincoln
```

32. (a) The Dewey Decimal System classifies books numerically:

000	General Works	500	Pure Science
100	Philosophy	600	Useful Arts
200	Religion	700	Fine Arts
300	Sociology	800	Literature
400	Philology	900	History

Note that the call or classification number of the book shown on the analytic card in No. 31 above is 920. Also note that the Dewey Decimal System reserves the 900 section for books on history.

(b) The Library of Congress System (used in large university libraries) classifies books according to the alphabet:

A	General Works	M–N	Fine Arts
B	Philosophy and religion	P	Language and literature
C–F	History and auxiliary science		
G	Geography and anthropology	Q	Science
H–K	Social and political sciences	R	Medicine
L	Education		

S	Agriculture	V	Naval science
T	Technology	Z	Biography and
U	Military science		library science

33. To ascertain whether any information on your topic is available in periodicals and newspapers, you would consult the many periodical and newspaper indexes available.

34. While periodical indexes may vary in style and arrangement, the following illustration shows the data usually given:

Readers' Guide to Periodical Literature. General periodicals by author and subject from 1900.

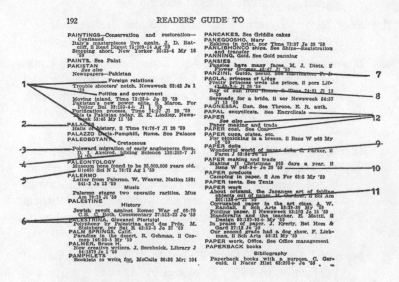

Courtesy of the H.W.Wilson Company

1 Subheading
2 Main heading
3 Title of article
4 Article contains bibliography
5 Article is illustrated
6 Author

7 Name of periodical
8 Volume number
9 Page number
10 Date of periodical
11 Article is continued in back of periodical
12 "See" and "see also" reference

35. Other important indexes which you should know about include:

   a. *Agricultural Index.* Agriculture, forestry, home economics, veterinary, and medicine listed by subject from 1916.

   b. *Applied Science and Technology Index.* Aeronautics, automation, chemistry, construction, electricity, and electrical communication, engineering, geology and metallurgy, industrial, and related subjects. Replaces the *Industrial Arts Index.*

   c. *Art Index.* Archeology, architecture, arts and crafts, ceramics, decoration and ornament, graphic arts, industrial design, interior decoration, landscape architecture, painting, sculpture. Subject index.

   d. *Book Review Digest.* "See" and "See also" references; 300 new subjects.

   e. *Business Periodicals Index.* Accounting, advertising, banking and finance, general business, insurance, labor and management, taxation, specific businesses, industries, and trades. Replaces the *Industrial Arts Index.* Subject index.

   f. *Education Index.* Child study, comparative education, curriculum development, educational psychology, educational research, elementary education, higher education, school administration, secondary education, statistical methods, teacher education, and related subjects. Author and subject index.

   g. *Industrial Arts Index.* Engineering, trade, businesses. Ceased publication in 1957. Replaced by *Applied Science and Technology Index* and the *Business Periodicals Index.* Subject index.

   h. *International Index.* Social sciences and humanities. Author and subject index.

   i. *The Times Index, London.* From 1886.

   j. *The New York Times Index.* People and events printed in the *New York Times.* Economics, sociology, and political science, from 1913.

k. *Poole's Index to Periodical Literature.* Articles listed by subject. Poems and stories listed by author and subject from 1802–1906. Service continued by *Readers' Guide.*

36. Book indexes list *all* books published. These indexes are arranged by author, subject, and title. This differs from your library card index, which lists only books found in your library.

37. The following are some of the more important book indexes:
a. Atlases (maps, geography, and economic information)
   Encyclopaedia Britannica World Atlas, 1954.
   Rand McNally Commercial Atlas and Marketing Guide, from 1935.
   Webster's Geographical Dictionary, 1955.

b. Biographical dictionaries
   Dictionary of American Biography. Important people in American history. 1928–37. Reprinted in 1943 and 1946.
   Dictionary of National Biography. Important people in English history. 1882–1910. Supplements to 1940.

c. Book lists
   Books in Print, 1948 to date. Annual.
   Subject Guide to Books in Print.

d. Books of quotations
   Familiar Quotations by Bartlett, 1955.
   Hoyt's New Cyclopedia of Practical Quotations, 1947.

e. Catalog
   United States Catalogue. Books published in the United States on a particular subject, 1928.

f. Cumulative Book Index
   Cumulative Book Index. Monthly supplements to the *United States Catalogue.* Includes all books published in the United States except textbooks and also includes books published and printed in the English language anywhere in the world. Listed by author, subject, and title. Useful in reading about subject when a book is not found in the local library.

g. Yearbooks (statistical information)
> *American Yearbook.* 1910–19, and from 1925.
> *Statesman's Year-book,* from 1864.
> *Statistical Abstract of the United States,* from 1878.
> *World Almanac and Book of Facts,* from 1868.

h. Miscellaneous
> *American Literature Index,* from 1929.
> *Cyclopedia of Education,* 1911–13.
> *Education Abstracts,* 1936–43.
> *Psychological Abstracts,* from 1954.
> *Psychological Index,* 1895–1931.
> *Review of Educational Research,* from 1931.

CHAPTER IV

PREPARING THE BIBLIOGRAPHY

Do not become overwhelmed by the abundance of material that may be available on your subject. Select your bibliography with care, so that it is not cluttered with references of little if any value to you. Spend considerable time on this bibliography because it will pay you dividends, not only in the opportunity it provides you to broaden your understanding and knowledge of your subject but also in the clues and ideas it offers which will help you develop your paper.

38. A working bibliography is a list of the sources of information selected by you.

39. The final bibliography appears at the end of the term paper and lists only those references that you use from your working bibliography.

40. Each reference in your working bibliography is recorded in ink on separate 3 by 5 cards.

Author's name
Title of reference
Facts of publication
    Edition
    Volume number
    Place of publication
    Name of publisher
    Date of publication
Comments (optional)

Current, Richard N.
Mr. Lincoln
N.Y.: Dodd, Mead and Co.
1957
[see page - 382 - Lincoln expresses his feelings about his own safety against would-be assassins.]

41. A typical term paper usually requires as many as 50 bibliographic references even though all are not included in the writing of the paper.

42. As you prepare your working bibliography, you will constantly be adding new cards and eliminating others.

43. By pruning, screening, adding, and dropping cards, your working bibliography develops into your final bibliography, which is a selected list of references far fewer in number than you originally had.

44. Examine appropriate books for information on your subject, quickly checking the table of contents, chapter headings, and index. Check for a bibliography at ends of chapters and at the end of the book.

45. After completing your first bibliography, prune or screen it by removing and placing in a separate pack the references which hold little promise of information about your subject. Save all cards in case you need the references later.

46. If a book reference holds promise, go to the card catalog and write the classification number in the upper left-hand corner of your 3 by 5 card.

47. If a periodical reference holds promise for you, check with your librarian to see if the library carries that particular magazine or newspaper.

> NOTE: In the bibliographic and footnote listings throughout the text of this book *italic type* is used for those items which should be underlined in your paper, since you are not expected to reproduce this type. You will see also that certain abbreviations and foreign expressions customarily appear in *italics,* both in this book and in your reading. Whenever you include such words in a paper, they should be underlined.

48. The proper form for listing references both for the working bibliographic cards and for the final bibliography for the term paper is illustrated below. The bibliography appears in alphabetical order with family name first at the end of the term paper.

Book

a. Anonymous works

  Textbooks Are Indispensable! New York: The American Textbook Publishers Institute, no date given.

b. One author

  Burlingame, Roger. *Endless Frontiers: The Story of McGraw-Hill.* New York: McGraw-Hill Book Co., Inc., 1959.

c. Two or three authors

  Wheeler, Jesse H. Jr., J. Trenton Kostbade, and Richard S. Thoman. *Regional Geography of the World.* New York: Henry Holt and Company, 1955.

d. More than three authors

  Deasy, George F., and others. *The World's Nations.* New York: J. B. Lippincott Company, 1958.

e. Edited work

  Peck, William T. (ed.). *Washington's Farewell Address and Webster's Bunker Hill Orations.* New York: The Macmillan Company, 1909.

f. Edited by a person other than the author

  Cooper, James Fenimore. *The Leatherstocking Saga,* ed. Allan Nevins. New York: Pantheon Books, 1954.

g. Edition other than the first

  Kimber, Diana Clifford, Carolyn E. Gray, and Caroline E. Stackpole. *Textbook of Anatomy and Physiology.* Eleventh edition. New York: The Macmillan Company, 1942.

h. Review

  Rolo, Charles. Review of *The Status Seekers,* by Vance Packard. *The Atlantic,* 203, (May 1959), p. 91.

i. Citing work in more than one volume

  Sawyer, Joseph Dillaway. *Washington.* 2 vols. New York: The Macmillan Company, 1927.

Encyclopedia article

j. Author listed

> Pickwell, Gayle. "Water Beetle," *The World Book Encyclopedia* (1950), 18: 8657–58.

k. No author listed

> "Mango," *Encyclopedia Americana* (1957), 23: 34–35.

Government document

l. Author listed

> Kellogg, Charles E. *We Seek to Learn* (U.S. Dept. of Agriculture, Yearbook on Soil). Washington: Government Printing Office, 1957.

m. No author listed

> *Statistical Abstract of the United States* (U.S. Dept. of Commerce, Bureau of the Census). Washington: Government Printing Office, 1958.

Newspaper article and editorial

n. Author listed

> Jones, Brendan M. "Soviet Trade Aim Worrying Canada," *New York Times,* September 20, 1959, Sec. 3, p. 1F, col. 8.

o. No author listed

> "Closed-Circuit TV Is Planned to Watch Apartment Elevators," *New York Times,* September 20, 1959, Sec. 8, p. 1R, col. 1.

p. "Strike Crisis," an editorial, (Albany, N.Y.) *Times Union,* September 26, 1959, Sec. 1, col. 1, p. 4.

Periodical article

q. Author listed

> Davidson, Sidney. "Diet and Cardiovascular Disease," *The American Journal of Nursing,* 57 (February, 1957), 194–6.

r. No author listed
> "Fifty Years of Progress in Distributive Education," *American Vocational Journal,* 31 (December, 1956), 271.

Miscellaneous

s. Essays, collection of
> Wilson, Edmund (ed.). *The Collected Essays of John Peale Bishop.* New York: Charles Scribner's Sons, 1948.

t. Interview
> Rockefeller, Nelson D. Governor of New York, Interview at the Executive Mansion, Albany (N.Y.), August 22, 1962, concerning juvenile delinquency.

u. Letter
> Custer, George A. A letter on file in the National Archives, Washington, D.C. [n.d.].

v. Pamphlet or bulletin in a series
> *Public Action for Powerful Schools,* Metropolitan School Study Council, Research Studies No. 3. New York: Bureau of Publications, Teachers College, Columbia University, 1949.

w. Quarterly
> Birdsall, Richard D. "Berkshire's Golden Age," *American Quarterly,* Vol. 8, Winter 1956, No. 4.

x. Unpublished doctoral dissertation
> Jelinek, Charles Frank. "I. The Synthesis of the Tetranydrocannabinol Homologs with Marihuana Activity. II. The Structure of Riddelliine." Unpublished doctoral dissertation in Chemistry, The Graduate School of the University of Illinois, Urbana, 1944.

y. Translation
> Koestler, Arthur. *Darkness at Noon,* trans. Daphne Hardy. New York: The Macmillan Company, 1952.

z. Yearbook article

Ojemann, Ralph H. "How to Work with Parents in Preventing Delinquency," *Juvenile Delinquency and the Schools,* pp. 172–90. Forty-seventh Yearbook of the National Society for the Study of Education, Part I. Chicago: University of Chicago Press, 1948.

CHAPTER V

TAKING NOTES

Once you have developed an adequate bibliography, you are ready to take notes. Here is the heart of your research, so do not hurry it. Be sure to write plainly in order to avoid transcription errors later, and include a source reference on each card to simplify your footnoting job (see Chapter VIII). Remember that the accuracy of the facts in your paper depends on the accuracy of your notes.

49. In the process of using your working bibliography, you make note of any information of value to your term paper.

50. Develop an orderly, systematic, and scholarly routine for note taking.

    It is important that you include all pertinent information such as complete reference to the source. Before you leave the source, double-check the reference and content for accuracy. This will save time hunting it up later.

51. You will take more notes than you need to complete your paper, but it is better to have too much information, which can be pruned for basic essentials, than to have so little that you must search for more at the last minute.

52. Be critical of what you read, and write sparingly, keeping your notes to a minimum.

53. The use of white lined cards for note taking makes it easy to sort, eliminate, and arrange data into logical sequence. It is not always possible to tell what is relevant as you take notes.

   Even though some of your notes may seem to have little value, do not dispose of them. Put them in a separate pack and label HOLD just in case you need them later.

54. Use a larger size card for note taking to avoid mix-up with the smaller bibliographic cards.

55. Carry spare cards with you at all times, as evidence sometimes presents itself in strange places.

56. Avoid unusual abbreviations as a form of shorthand in note taking, for you run the risk of failing to transcribe accurately, particularly when a quotation is involved.

57. Write on one side of the card. If you must continue onto a second card, write "continued" at the top and label each card A and B.

58. Place only one idea on each card.

See No. 59.

59. Notes may be of the following types: quotation, paraphrase, personal comment.

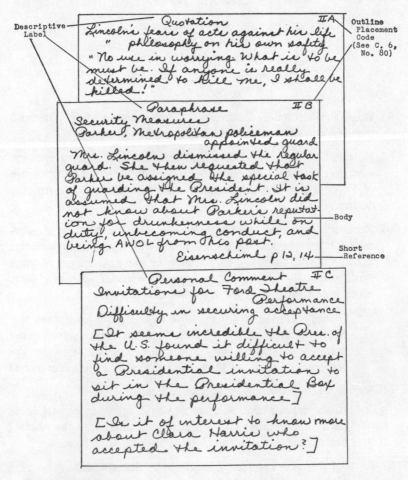

Descriptive Label

Outline Placement Code (See C. 6, No. 80)

Body

Short Reference

Quotation II A
Lincoln's fears of acts against his life
" philosophy on his own safety
"No use in worrying. What is to be must be. If anyone is really determined to kill me, I shall be killed!"

Paraphrase II B
Security Measures
Parker, Metropolitan policeman appointed guard
Mrs. Lincoln dismissed the regular guard. She then requested that Parker be assigned the special task of guarding the President. It is assumed that Mrs. Lincoln did not know about Parker's reputation for drunkenness while on duty, unbecoming conduct, and being AWOL from his past.
Eisenschiml p 12, 14

Personal Comment II C
Invitations for Ford Theatre Performance
Difficulty in securing acceptance
[It seems incredible the Pres. of the U.S. found it difficult to find someone willing to accept a Presidential invitation to sit in the Presidential Box during the performance]
[Is it of interest to know more about Clara Harris who accepted the invitation?]

60. At the top center of each card, on the red line, write the type of note you are making.

See No. 59.

61. Each card should have a descriptive label consisting of a main heading and subheading.

See No. 59.

62. Each card contains three essential items of information:
Reference to the source
Descriptive label
Body

See No. 59.

63. Read the reference thoroughly before writing your note and then digest what you have read into one key idea.

64. Notes which summarize, comment upon the text, and/or evaluate what you have read are superior to quotation notes because more of YOU is put into the paper and that is what your instructor desires.

65. Recording essential information when you are reading a reference for the purpose of taking notes will save you time later. Then you will not have to go back in the final stages of your work when you are writing or typing the paper to obtain facts which are so easily obtainable during note taking.

Identify sources of information in the short form (see No. 59 paraphrase card) by including the author's last name unless your bibliography lists more than one book by the same name, or more than one person with the same name.

66. Identify facts and opinions in your notes.

If the author expresses a personal opinion, record it as such in your notes and preface his opinion with the phrase, "according to the author," or some similar phrase.

67. Facts of common knowledge need not be documented.

Such statements as "Columbus discovered America in 1492" and "Henry Hudson sailed up the Hudson River" are common knowledge and need not be documented or carry a footnote reference.

68. Statements (a) which have questionable validity and/or (b) are controversial in nature, and/or (c) which contain little-known facts must be documented.

    a. Statements open to question should be documented. For example, if you were to use the statement, "Smoking is a prime cause of cancer," it would be necessary and important to know who said it, since the medical profession is divided on the subject.

    b. A controversial statement, such as "Smoking causes stunted growth," needs to be documented.

    c. A little-known fact, such as "Contrary to popular belief, the Indians who massacred General Custer and his 7th Cavalry were armed for the most part with bows and arrows while only a few Indians were equipped with repeater rifles," should be documented.

69. Laws and formulas should appear as quotations.

70. Copy quotations exactly including punctuation, spelling, capitalization, paragraphing, and errors.

71. Use quotations only when you wish to retain the exact wording of the author because his statement is not clear, is of great significance, or is of a challenging nature.

72. Ellipses are used to indicate the omission of a few words from a quotation when such omissions are irrelevant to your subject.

    a. Use three spaced dots when the omission is at the beginning or in the middle of a sentence.

    b. Use three spaced dots plus a period (four spaced dots) when the omission occurs at the end of a sentence.

    SEE TERM PAPER PAGE 8.

73. When ellipses end a quotation, place the ellipses inside the quotation mark.

74. Indicate the omission of an entire paragraph or more by a full line of doubled spaced periods (ellipses).

    SEE TERM PAPER PAGE 8.

75. When you wish to insert your own words within a quotation, place brackets [ ] around your words.

SEE TERM PAPER PAGE 3.

76. If you note an error in your reference and you wish to call this error to the attention of your reader, copy the quotation exactly as it appears in the original, follow the error with the word *sic* placed in brackets, and then make the correction.

77. Keep your completed notes on file until your term paper has been returned by your instructor.

CHAPTER VI

MAKING THE OUTLINE

After you have prepared your note cards, you are ready to make your first outline. It may be necessary to revise this outline several times. Work it out with great care, for you are only one step away from writing the first draft of your paper.

78. An outline enumerates important ideas to be developed in the paper.

79. An outline keeps you from wandering by forcing you to clarify your thinking about your subject.

   As your outline comes into focus, gaps in your research (note card information) will be apparent and you will then see where additional research is needed.

80. There is a relationship between the outline and the note cards.

   The usual procedure is to base the outline on the note cards. It is better to prepare the outline after the notes have been completed, even though it *is* possible to prepare the outline before taking your notes. Refer to the three note cards in No. 59. The outline placement code appearing in the upper right-hand corner of each card was placed there as a result of having arranged the note cards in some order. The quotation card was assigned the code IIA, the paraphrase card was given the outline code IIB, and the personal comment card was assigned IIC.

   See No. 59 and the topic and sentence outline in No. 90.

81. If you prepare your outline from your notes, you may want to spread your note cards on the floor and put them back together again in logical order.

82. An outline should provide a guide for writing a term paper. It may list items in their order of time occurrence.

    If the term paper is on Lincoln's assassination, your *first* outline might appear as follows:

    LINCOLN'S ASSASSINATION
    I.   Before the assassination
    II. The assassination
    III. After the assassination

83. An outline may also develop by expanding the main thought without regard to chronological arrangement.

    LINCOLN'S ASSASSINATION—AN UNSOLVED MYSTERY
    I.   The act itself
    II. Grant's strange behavior
    III. Mrs. Lincoln's unfortunate choice of bodyguard
    IV. The President's premonition
    V.   Booth's strange revelations

84. Your outline can change to suit your purpose. You are not shackled to the first one you prepare. Constant revision of your outline will develop it to full maturity.

    Note how the outlines on Lincoln's assassination in Nos. 82, 83, 88, and the topic outline in 90 change as they mature.

85. The outline must indicate a reason for your paper. It must show relationships between facts, and it must come to a logical conclusion.

    Avoid words like Introduction, Body, and Summary in your outline. They are vague and do not contribute to the development of your paper. Specific headings are needed.

86. Avoid too many main headings but have at least three.

The following outline form illustrates too fine a breakdown:

I.

    A.

        1.

        2.

           a.

           b.

               (1)

               (2)

                   (a)

                   (b)

                       ((1))

                       ((2))

    B.

87. If you list a I, you must also have a II. This is true for all subdivisions.

88. All main headings such as I, II, and III should be of the same value.

Unequal headings	*Equal headings*
LINCOLN'S ASSASSINATION	LINCOLN'S ASSASSINATION
I. Events leading to the murder	I. Events leading to the murder
II. The murder	II. The murder
III. Confusing news reports	III. Booth's escape
IV. Sgt. Cobb	IV. Booth's accomplices
V. Patrolman Parker	

89. Have all periods in main heading numbers line up. This also applies to all subdivisions.

90. Although a topic outline is easier to prepare, a sentence outline is preferred because it makes the writer really think about his subject and will result in an easier task and a superior paper.

Notice in the following partial outlines how the sentence outline brings the student closer to the point of writing his paper.

TOPIC OUTLINE

LINCOLN'S ASSASSINATION—A MURDER MYSTERY

I. Purpose of the paper
II. Lincoln—before the assassination
    A. His premonition of approaching death
        1. Dreams
        2. Philosophy
        3. Conversations
    B. His lack of security protection
        1. Unreliable personal bodyguard
        2. Lock on theater presidential box broken
        3. Peep hole bored through box door undetected
    C. His difficulty in obtaining guests for the performance
        1. Grant to be honored with Lincoln at theater
        2. Grant accepts President's invitation
        3. Grant declines invitation
        4. Lincoln finds himself without guests
III. The assassination
    A. A look at the assassin
    B. Motives for murder
    C. The shooting
    D. Stanton's famous last words
IV. After the assassination
    A. Booth's escape into Maryland
        1. Passed through guard post
        2. Received medical aid from physician
        3. Hidden by southern sympathizers

      B. Stanton's lack of co-operation
          1. Refused to give Booth's name to press
          2. Disinterested in capture of John Surrat
      C. The accomplices
      D. The trial

The final outline appears in sentence form. Every heading and subdivision is a complete statement.

SENTENCE OUTLINE

LINCOLN'S ASSASSINATION—A MURDER MYSTERY

I. The purpose of this paper is to identify unexplained events in connection with the death of Abraham Lincoln.

      A. Records of the assassination reveal gaps and inconsistencies of the events leading up to and following the murder.

      B. John Wilkes Booth killed Lincoln, but why he did it and the full details of his diabolical plan leave many questions unanswered.

II. Lincoln had been marked for death by several people during his term in office, but efforts to protect his life went unnoticed.

      A. Before his death, Lincoln had suspected that he would be killed at the hands of an assassin.

          1. He was extremely melancholy on the day of the shooting, having been troubled by bad dreams.

          2. His philosophy on his own safety reflected a fatalistic attitude.

          3. He said "goodbye" rather than "goodnight" as he left the White House for the theater.

   B. The President was not provided with ade-
       quate security measures.
            1. The regular guard was dismissed
                and a discredited police officer was
                assigned to guard his life.
                 a. Patrolman Parker had been
                     officially reprimanded for
                     drunkenness on several occa-
                     sions.
                 b. Parker had been found guilty
                     of conduct unbecoming an
                     officer on several occasions.
                 c. Parker had been known to
                     leave his post without proper
                     leave on several occasions.
            2. The lock on the door leading to
                the presidential box was broken.
            3. A peep hole that had been bored
                in the door leading to the presi-
                dential box went unnoticed.

91. If asked, submit your outline to your instructor for his approval.
    You may save yourself time and heartache.

Chapter VII

WRITING THE PAPER

Very few people are naturally gifted writers. For most of us, writing is a difficult task. To do a creditable job it will be necessary for you to rework paragraphs and labor over some of your sentences as you try to find the word that expresses the precise thought you have in mind. Above all, do not get discouraged now. Others are going through the same experience and those who persevere and rise above their discouragements will finally achieve their goal, a term paper of which they can be proud.

92. Do not delay writing until the last possible moment. You cannot do a good job if you rush it. Allow yourself ample time.

93. Keep within the number of words set for your paper by your instructor.

A minimum of 2000 words is usually required.

94. Choose a final title that is interesting, clear, and brief.

SEE TERM PAPER TITLE PAGE.

95. Your instructor will probably be influenced by your opening and closing paragraphs, so make them especially good.

96. Not even the most experienced writer can hope that his first draft will be his best draft.

Prepare yourself to write several drafts before your paper is in its final form.

97. During your first draft, start writing and do not be concerned with grammar or sentence construction. You can correct this later. The important thing is to *get started*.

98. Avoid merely copying your notes. This makes the reading dull, choppy, and lacks the most essential element, YOU.

99. Avoid colloquialisms and slang expressions.

100. If you have a choice between using a simple word or a technical one, choose the simpler word your reader will understand.

   His remuneration for the week was in excess of $200.
   His pay for the week was more than $200.

101. Try to avoid making any personal references to yourself such as *I, me, mine,* or *the writer.* Keep personal pronouns out of the paper if possible.

102. Have a dictionary and a thesaurus handy and consult them.

103. Write the first draft with your notes and outline before you. Use the outline as your writing guide and your notes to recall the facts. Do not write your paper by copying your notes.

104. Use wide margins and triple space your first draft to allow room for corrections.

105. Use separate sheets of paper for each paragraph in your draft. This will allow you to add to your paragraphs during your revision and to insert footnotes without fear of crowding your work.

106. Write or type on one side of 8½- by 11-inch paper which is of quality good enough to take erasing and editing.

107. Prepare a carbon copy in case your instructor wishes to see your draft. Term papers *have* been lost.

108. If asked, submit a clean copy of your revised draft to your instructor. Type it if possible.

109. Allow one-half inch (three lines) for each footnote.

110. Documenting and footnoting are closely related. To document means to cite quotations in the text; to footnote means to list the exact reference of the quotation.

SEE TERM PAPER PAGE 8.

111. Document and footnote as you write your draft. You might forget one or the other if you hold off doing this until your final copy is being prepared. (See Chapter VIII for the form and content of footnotes.)

112. When using a quotation, work it into the text smoothly with a transitional sentence.

SEE TERM PAPER PAGE 9.

113. Quoted matter should not take up more than one fifth of your paper. The remainder of your text comes from your own ideas.

114. Long quotations do not have quotation marks, are single spaced and indented five spaces from the left and right margins of the context.

SEE TERM PAPER PAGE 11.

115. Rather than copying a quotation, staple or clip the quotation note card to your draft. This saves time and ensures against an error during the copying.

116. Avoid using quoted matter unless it is absolutely essential that the words of another be included.

117. Acknowledge all paraphrases by using a superscript after the material and then listing it in the footnotes. Don't pass someone else's ideas off as your own.

SEE TERM PAPER PAGE 6.

118. Determine whether the paragraphs of your first draft are in logical order. If not, change them.

119. Every paragraph should have a key, or topic sentence—usually at its beginning.

120. Have medium and short paragraphs for interest.

121. If you include a summary paragraph, it should be short and concise and should answer the question in your opening paragraph, if that is the way your paper begins.

122. After your first writing, lay the paper aside and let it "cook" in your mind. Then when your outlook is fresh, pick it up and criticize it ruthlessly. It is far better for you to do this than to have the criticisms come from your instructor.

123. Internally examine the paper for unity, coherence, and structure. Ask yourself:

    Does the central theme hold together well?
    Does the paper express itself clearly?
    Is the paper well put together grammatically?

    Other questions which will help you evaluate your paper can be found in the term paper checklist preceding the sample term paper.

124. It may be necessary for you to clip and paste your first draft in different order for a more logical arrangement.

    From your pasted draft, prepare your final copy.

125. Review and edit the final draft before typing the copy which you will submit to your instructor. This means that you must correct grammar, switch paragraphs, change words, delete irrelevant material, sharpen sentences to pinpoint thoughts, and add appropriate tables.

126. Check all footnotes and bibliographic entries for consistency of form and to see that all essential information is included.

127. Through constant pruning of irrelevant material, you may find your final copy shorter than your draft.

128. If the final copy sounds like a learned academician rather than like you, this difference will also be noted by your instructor. Now is the time to make changes that will reflect your own personality rather than to submit a paper that sounds like someone who possesses a number of college degrees.

129. The finished paper should include a title page, table of contents (optional), text, and a bibliography, in that order.

SEE TERM PAPER.

130. If a table of contents is needed, your outline, slightly revised, will serve the purpose.

131. Place your completed paper in a folder. Type a label giving the title of your paper, your name, name and number of the course, the instructor's name, and the date.

132. Remove from your note cards material you do not use in the paper and keep these extra notes securely bound in a separate pack.

133. Save your note cards, since your instructor may wish to examine them.

134. If you mount illustrations in your paper, use rubber cement to prevent wrinkling.

135. If tables are to be included in your paper, remember that their only purpose is to communicate ideas, so make them brief and simple.

See No. 137.

136. Each table should present only one idea.

See No. 137.

TABLE I

VIEWING HOURS PER WEEK OF TELEVISION PROGRAMS BY TYPE

Type	*Hours Per Week*
Audience participation contests	3
Music	5
Panel shows	2
Sports	1
Variety	7
Western movies	3

137. Make each table so simple that its meaning is immediately clear to the reader.

138. Introduce each table with a brief transitional sentence.

139. Number each table consecutively throughout the paper.
     Use capital roman numerals.
     See No. 137.

140. Every table must have a simple title which appears in capital letters two spaces under the table number. Do not include as part of the table title words such as "Table Showing."

141. If numbers in the table are rounded off, be sure to inform your reader.

142. If you draw lines in your table, use a ruler with a steel edge, a pen with a fine point, and black ink for greater contrast.

143. Avoid splitting a long table onto two pages. It is better to place it on one page and insert it as close to the contextual matter as possible.

Chapter VIII

FOOTNOTING

Footnotes add authority to what you say and are a vital part of your paper's documentation. Where they are used, accuracy, completeness, and consistency should prevail.

You will want to refer to Chapter IV to see how footnote form differs from bibliographic form.

144. Footnotes have two purposes:
   a. To cite exact page references for quoted matter
   b. To provide additional interesting information which is pertinent but not of primary importance.
See term paper page 4.

145. Footnotes may be *simple* or *formal,* depending upon the wishes of your instructor, the style followed by your college, and the level of research undertaken in the paper.
See Nos. 146 and 147.

146. The simplified footnote style merely lists (a) the last name of the author, the title, and the exact page reference, or (b) the title, the reference, and page if the work is anonymous.
Examples of simple style:
   a. [1]Current, *Mr. Lincoln,* p. 382.
   b. [2]"Assassination," *The World Book Encyclopedia,* p. 4472.

147. The formal footnote style lists the full name (in proper order with family name last), title, place of publication, publisher, date, volume number, and the exact page to which reference is made.

Example of formal footnote style:

[1]Richard N. Current, *Mr. Lincoln* (New York: Dodd, Mead and Co., 1957), p. 382.

SEE TERM PAPER PAGE 2.
See No. 158 of this chapter.

148. The major purpose of a footnote is to refer the reader to the exact page reference. If your reader is satisfied with this and is content to get more detailed information in the bibliography at the end of the term paper, use the simplified style. If this style is annoying to the reader, use the formal type of footnote. Check with your instructor first.

149. A footnote cites the exact page reference, but the bibliography provides complete information about the reference. Every footnote must also have a bibliographic reference.

SEE TERM PAPER PAGE 3 AND BIBLIOGRAPHY.

150. Footnotes are punctuated like sentences. Phrases within them are separated by commas and they end with periods.

SEE TERM PAPER PAGE 3.

151. Footnoting is a distraction to the reader. Avoid over-footnoting.

152. There are three acceptable methods for numbering footnotes:
   a. Continuous numbering throughout the paper
   b. Continuous numbering within each chapter
   c. Continuous numbering by page with each page starting with number 1.

   The sample term paper at the end of this manual follows the style of (a) for footnoting.

153. Place the footnote on the same page as the material being cited.

SEE TERM PAPER PAGE 4.

154. If a footnote must be carried over to the next page, break the footnote in the middle of the sentence and complete it at the

bottom of the next page in the footnote position. Avoid breaking footnotes.

155. The number appearing at the beginning of the footnote is called an index number or superscript. Although it may be typed on the line, most style manuals suggest its being placed one-half space above the line.

SEE TERM PAPER PAGE 5.

156. The index number or superscript appearing at the end of the matter in the context appears one-half space above the line. This index number is the same as the superscript number of the footnote to which it refers.

SEE TERM PAPER PAGE 5.

157. The first line of the footnote is indented one-half inch from the left margin. All other lines for that footnote are even with the margin.

SEE TERM PAPER PAGE 4.

158. Footnotes are single spaced and separated by double spaces.

SEE TERM PAPER PAGE 9.

159. There are two ways of separating the text from the footnotes:
    a. A solid line of underscores 1½ inches long extending from the left margin.

    SEE TERM PAPER PAGE 6.

    b. A solid line of underscores extending from the left margin to the right margin.

    The sample term paper uses the style described in (a).

160. Type the line of underscores either for (a) or (b) above, one or two spaces below the last line of context on the page but be consistent. Use the shift and 6 keys for making the underscores.

SEE TERM PAPER PAGE 6.

161. Allow a minimum of one-half inch (3 lines) for every footnote. This allowance provides for the material as well as for the blank line above and below it.

162. Short cuts may be used to save time when more than one footnote refers to the same work.

    The use of the Latin terms *ibid, loc. cit.,* and *op. cit.* help abbreviate the footnoting task.

    Although there is a trend away from the use of Latin terms in footnoting, you will come upon such terms in your reading, and you should know what they mean.

163. *Ibid.* refers to the immediately preceding footnote. It replaces the author's name and the title when both are the same as in the preceding footnote.

    SEE TERM PAPER PAGE 6.

164. *Loc. cit.* refers to the same reference. It is used when other footnotes intervene. *Loc. cit.* is preceded by the author's name. Do not give the page number when using *loc. cit.*

    SEE TERM PAPER PAGE 5.

165. *Op. cit.* refers to the work cited. It eliminates the need for the title of the work. The author's name precedes *op. cit.* and the page references follow it. Use *op. cit.* when there are intervening footnotes. *Op. cit.* cites the same work but refers to a different page.

    SEE TERM PAPER PAGE 7.

166. By making use of Latin terms, footnotes may appear as follows:
    [4]Hervey Allen, *The City in the Dawn* (New York: Rinehart and Co., Inc., 1950), p. 58.
    [5]*Ibid.,* p. 149 (refers to footnote 4).

    SEE TERM PAPER PAGE 8.

    [6]*Ibid.* (refers to footnote 5).
    [7]Bruce Bliven, *The Wonderful Writing Machine* (New York: Random House, 1954), p. 52.
    [8]Allen, *op. cit.,* p. 161. (Refers to work cited in footnote 4 but on a different page.)

    SEE TERM PAPER PAGE 6.

    [9]Bliven, *loc. cit.* (Refers to footnote 7, same work, same page.)

    SEE TERM PAPER PAGE 5.

167. If you refer to more than one work by the same author, in every case you must include the author's name, book title, and the page number.

168. Common types of footnotes include the following:

Book

a. Anonymous works
    [1] *Textbooks Are Indispensable!* (New York: The American Textbook Publishers Institute, [n.d.]), p. 32.

b. One author
    [2]Roger Burlingame, *Endless Frontiers: The Story of McGraw-Hill* (New York: McGraw-Hill Book Co., Inc., 1959), p. 110.

c. Two or three authors
    [3]Jesse H. Wheeler, Jr., J. Trenton Kosbade, and Richard S. Thoman, *Regional Geography of the World* (New York: Henry Holt and Company, 1955), p. 32.

d. More than three authors
    [4]George F. Deasy and others, *The World's Nations* (New York: J. B. Lippincott Company, 1958), p. 415.

e. Edited work
    [5]William T. Peck (ed.), *Washington's Farewell Address and Webster's Bunker Hill Orations* (New York: The Macmillan Company, 1909), pp. 17–26.

f. Edited by a person other than the author
    [6]James Fenimore Cooper, *The Leatherstocking Saga,* ed. Allan Nevins (New York: Pantheon Books, 1954), p. 352.

g. Edition other than the first
    [7]Diana Clifford Kimber, Carolyn E. Gray, and Caroline E. Stackpole, *Textbook of Anatomy and Physiology* (eleventh edition. New York: The Macmillan Company, 1942), pp. 24–29.

h. Review
    [8]Charles Rolo, Review of *The Status Seekers* by Vance Packard, *The Atlantic,* 203, (May, 1959), 91.

i. Citing work in more than one volume
> [9]Joseph Dillaway Sawyer, *Washington,* 2 vols. (New York: The Macmillan Company, 1927), pp. 36–39 of vol. 1.

Encyclopedia article

j. Author listed
> [10]Gayle Pickwell, "Water Beetle," *The World Book Encyclopedia* (1950), 18: 8657–58.

k. No author listed
> [11]"Mango," *Encyclopedia Americana* (1957), 23: 34–35.

Government document

l. Author listed
> [12]Charles E. Kellogg, *We Seek to Learn,* U.S. Department of Agriculture, Yearbook on Soil (Washington: Government Printing Office, 1957), pp. 32–86.

m. No author listed
> [13]U.S. Department of Commerce, Bureau of the Census, *Statistical Abstract of the United States.* (Washington: Government Printing Office, 1958), p. 101.

Newspaper article and editorial

n. Author listed
> [14]Brendan M. Jones, "Soviet Trade Aim Worrying Canada," *New York Times,* September 20, 1959, Sec. 3, p. 1F, col. 8.

o. No author listed
> [15]"Closed-Circuit TV Is Planned to Watch Apartment Elevators," *New York Times,* September 20, 1959, Sec. 8, p. 1R, col. 1.

p. Editorial
> [16]"Strike Crisis," an editorial. Albany (Albany, N.Y.) *Times Union,* September 26, 1959, Sec. 1, col. 1, p. 4.

Periodical article

q. Author listed
>   [17]Sidney Davidson, "Diet and Cardiovascular Disease," *The American Journal of Nursing,* 57 (February, 1957), 194–96.

r. No author listed
>   [18]"Fifty Years of Progress in Distributive Education," *American Vocational Journal,* 31 (December, 1956), 271.

Miscellaneous

s. Essays, collection of
>   [19]Edmund Wilson (ed.), "The Collected Essays of John Peale Bishop," (New York: Charles Scribner's Sons, 1948), p. 14.

t. Interview
>   [20]Nelson D. Rockefeller, Governor of New York, *Interview at Executive Mansion,* Albany (N.Y.), August 22, 1962, concerning juvenile delinquency.

u. Letter
>   [21]Letter written by George A. Custer on file in the National Archives (Washington, D.C.), [n.d.].

v. Pamphlet or bulletin in a series
>   [22]*Public Action for Powerful Schools* (Teachers College, Columbia University, Metropolitan School Study Council, Research Studies No. 3, New York: Bureau of Publications, 1949), p. 17.

w. Quarterly
>   [23]Richard D. Birdsall, "Berkshire's Golden Age," *American Quarterly,* Vol. 8, Winter 1956, No. 4, pp. 328–55.

x. Unpublished doctoral dissertation
>   [24]Charles Frank Jelinek, "I. The Synthesis of the Tetranydrocannabinol Homologs with Marihuana Activity. II. The Structure of Riddelliine." Unpublished doctoral dissertation in Chemistry, The Graduate School of the University of Illinois, Urbana, Illinois, 1944, p. 27.

y. Translation

[25] Arthur Koestler, *Darkness at Noon,* trans. Daphne Hardy (New York: The Macmillan Company, 1952), p. 31.

z. Yearbook article

[26] Ralph H. Ojemann, "How to Work with Parents in Preventing Delinquency," *Juvenile Delinquency and the Schools,* Forty-seventh Yearbook of the National Society for the Study of Education, Part I. (Chicago: University of Chicago Press, 1948), p. 185.

Chapter IX

TYPING THE PAPER

The end is in sight, but don't spoil all you have done by passing in your paper prematurely. Although you may have a very legible handwriting, it is always easier to read from type than from longhand. Besides, the extra effort you exert at this time by getting your paper typed may be reflected in the grade you receive from the person who reads it. Put yourself in the reader's position: Wouldn't you react favorably to a typed paper after "wading" through a number of other papers, many of which may be written in longhand? Do yourself a special favor and submit a clean, neatly set up, *typed* paper.

169. Unless your instructor specifies otherwise, follow the general style suggestions offered in this manual.

170. If you plan to bind your paper in a folder, purchase the folder before typing your paper, because it will influence the margins you will have.

171. Type on white, 8½- by 11-inch bond, of good quality such as a 20-pound weight and a high rag content. This will give you an attractive, typed copy.

172. Type or write on one side of the paper.

173. If you handwrite your paper, use white paper with ruled lines approximately one-half inch apart.

174. Black ink is preferred when handwriting your paper and when making corrections on the final copy. Make corrections in small print above the line.

175. If your final copy has more than two or three errors a page, write or type the page over to create a more finished effect.

176. If someone else is going to type your term paper, go over the handwritten draft with the typist to clear up the spellings of words where your writing may be indistinguishable. This is especially important for quoted matter and footnotes.

177. Lend this manual to your typist to use as a guide in typing your paper, paying particular attention to this chapter and also to the sample term paper.

178. Retain a carbon copy for your files.

179. After inserting the pack (first sheet, carbon, and second sheet) into your typewriter, check to see that it is in proper order.

   Peel back the first page. If you see the *dull* side of the carbon, your pack is inserted correctly. Do this every time you insert a new pack.

180. After inserting your pack, be sure to remove wrinkles in the carbon paper before typing.

   Release the paper release lever by pulling it toward you. The lever is on the right side of the typewriter next to the cylinder knob. Avoid disturbing the pack. Gently run your thumbnail across the paper over the cylinder. Move your paper release back to its original position *away* from you.

181. If you type your paper, use a fresh black ribbon to give your paper the best possible appearance.

182. Use a cleaning agent (fluid, special putty, or blotters) to clean your typewriter keys. No one likes to read a typed paper in which the individual letters such as *a, o, d, b, c, p,* or *e* are clogged or completely filled because of dirty typewriter bars.

183. It makes little difference whether you use an elite- or a pica-style type for your paper. Avoid using script or micro, since they are more difficult to read.

184. A typewriter with elite type has a scale just below the cylinder which usually reads from 0 to 115. A pica scale usually reads from 0 to 95. Both machines have 6 lines to the vertical inch. Therefore, a paper 11 inches long has 66 lines.

185. If your paper is not going to be enclosed in a folder, use a left margin of 1½ inches and a right margin of one inch. Measure this with a ruler. Place dots at the top of the paper for the left and right margins. Insert your paper into the typewriter and move your marginal stops to the dots.

186. If your paper will have a cover, you may need a left margin of two inches.

187. To be sure you have enough room for footnotes on your page, follow this procedure:

Immediately after typing the superscript or index number in your contextual matter, roll down to the one-inch mark at the bottom of your paper. Then roll up three spaces and place a new mark at this point to indicate your last line of contextual matter. Roll up to the contextual matter and continue typing until you come to your second superscript. Follow the same procedure of marking your paper at the bottom by spacing up three more lines from the highest pencil mark.

188. On all pages, other than page 1, have a top margin of one inch (six lines). Start typing on the seventh line.

SEE TERM PAPER PAGE 2.

189. Set your machine for double spacing. Double spacing means that you have one blank line between every typed line.

190. The body of the term paper is double spaced, but quotations longer than three or four lines, footnotes, and the bibliography are single spaced. Long quotations and footnotes are indented 5 spaces from the left margin of the contextual matter. Long quotations are also indented 5 spaces from the right contextual margin.

SEE TERM PAPER PAGE 3.

191. If a long quotation takes more than one paragraph, double space between paragraphs.

192. Underscore only words and not the space between words in book titles.

193. Titles of articles in periodicals are not underscored but are enclosed in quotation marks.

See No. 168 q and r.

194. Double space between each footnote.

See term paper page 8.

195. Double space between each bibliographic entry. If the bibliographic entry requires more than one line, all lines after the first are indented 5 spaces.

See term paper bibliography.

196. It is all right to be one line over or under your bottom margin but any more of a variance will result in a "short" page or a crowded page.

197. Avoid the use of thesis paper for an undergraduate written assignment. The use of such papers may be interpreted as putting on airs. Use plain bond.

198. Make underscores according to one of the methods explained in number 159. Use the shift and 6 keys.

199. Type the line of underscoring either one or two spaces below the last line of context on the page but be consistent.

See term paper page 8.

200. Use the small *l* key for making a figure 1 as in 1960. Your typewriter may have a figure 1 key on the top row. If so, use it. Do not use the capital I for the figure 1.

201. The title page gives the title of your paper, the word "by," your name, the name of the course, the course number, your instructor's name, and the date you submit the report, in that order.

See term paper.

202. The title may be typed in capitals or in lower case on your title page. Use the form preferred by your instructor.

SEE TERM PAPER.

203. Avoid any decorative designs on the title page.

204. If an outline is to be submitted with the paper, it comes immediately after the title page.

205. The outline is numbered with a small i at the bottom center exactly one inch (6 lines) from the bottom.

206. If your outline requires two pages, the second page is numbered ii at the bottom.

207. The first page of your contextual matter is not numbered, although it does count as page 1. All succeeding pages are numbered in the upper right corner in the same position so that if you were to flip all your numbered pages rapidly, you would see them dance before your eyes. Numbers should appear one inch from the right margin, and 3 lines from the top of the paper.

SEE TERM PAPER PAGE 2.

208. If the title of your term paper is also to appear on page 1, place it three inches (18 lines) from the top and center it. If you write your paper, the title appears without underscoring and in small letters. If your paper is typed, the title appears in capitalized form.

SEE TERM PAPER.

209. Space down three lines after the title to begin the first line of your paper.

SEE TERM PAPER.

210. If your paper has subheadings, underline the words but not the spaces.

SEE TERM PAPER PAGE 2.

211. A footnote is preceded by a raised number. This number is the same as the superscript or index number in the contextual matter on the same page.

SEE TERM PAPER PAGE 11.

212. Footnotes are single spaced, with a double space between footnotes.

SEE TERM PAPER PAGE 11.

213. There are three acceptable methods for numbering footnotes.

See No. 152.

214. Although it is possible to complete a footnote at the bottom of the next page, it is better to retype the page and get the complete footnote on the page where it belongs.

215. Indent 5 spaces for the first line of paragraphs and footnotes.

216. If you quote poetry, separate it from your text matter by indenting and single spacing it.

217. If you include a quotation within a quotation, the inside quotation has single quotation marks while the outside quotation has double quotes.

218. Commas and periods appear inside the quotation marks.

SEE TERM PAPER PAGE 9.

219. The bibliography constitutes the last page, or pages, of your term paper.

220. Only references which you use in your paper may be included in your bibliography.

221. Type the word BIBLIOGRAPHY in capital letters at the top center of the first page on which the bibliography appears.

SEE TERM PAPER BIBLIOGRAPHY.

222. While footnotes have the author's name in signature order, the name is reversed in the bibliography.

SEE TERM PAPER PAGE 2 AND BIBLIOGRAPHY.

223. Arrange your bibliography in alphabetic order.

SEE TERM PAPER BIBLIOGRAPHY.

224. Proofread your final copy.

225. If you submit your paper in loose form, without staples or clips, type your name (last name first) in the upper right corner, followed by the page number on each page. Avoid submitting your paper in this form.

226. If you submit your paper in a folder, be sure your folder carries a label on the outside.

TERM PAPER CHECKLIST

	Yes	No
1. Does my introductory paragraph get the paper off to a flying start?	——	——
2. Does the introductory section state specifically the purpose of my paper?	——	——
3. Have I developed the body of the paper according to the outline?	——	——
4. Does each paragraph link up with the previous and following paragraphs?	——	——
5. Does each paragraph have one central thought?	——	——
6. Are the lengths of my sentences varied to avoid monotony?	——	——
7. Have I refrained from drawing too much material from one source?	——	——
8. Does the language sound like my own?	——	——
9. Have I eliminated meanderings and unnecessary repetitions?	——	——
10. Does the paper accomplish my objective as stated in the opening paragraph?	——	——
11. Do my conclusions rest on the evidence presented in the paper?	——	——
12. Do any comments of my own stem from my findings?	——	——

13. As I read it over, is my paper clear, does it make sense? ___ ___

14. Is it interesting to read? ___ ___

15. Does the paper reflect my best effort? ___ ___

16. Is my paper's physical presentation neat and attractive? ___ ___

17. Is it grammatically free from errors? ___ ___

18. Have I proofread the paper to double-check spelling and punctuation? ___ ___

19. Are the pages, except page 1, numbered in the upper right-hand corner in the correct order? ___ ___

20. Have I checked the accuracy of my quoted material? ___ ___

21. Are short quotations of three or four lines or less enclosed in quotation marks and run in with the contextual matter? ___ ___

22. Are longer quotations indented and set off in single-spaced type with no quotation marks? ___ ___

23. Does each quotation carry a footnote reference? ___ ___

24. Is the bibliography in correct form? ___ ___

25. Is one method of numbering footnotes used consistently throughout the paper? ___ ___

26. Have I double-checked the accuracy of these footnotes? ___ ___

27. Is every source mentioned in a footnote included in the bibliography? ___ ___

Abbreviations Commonly Used in Reference Books

A.D.	after the birth of Christ (*Anno Domini,* in the year of our Lord)
ad loc.	at the passage cited (*ad locum,* to or at the place)
art.	article
aet.	italicized (*aetatis,* of age)
anon.	anonymous
ante	before
B.C.	before Christ
bibliog.	bibliography
b.	born
bk.	book
C. or ©	copyright
ca.	about (*circa*)
cf.	confer
cf. ante	compare above
cf. post	compare below
chap.	chapter
col.	column
comp.	compiled, -er
diss.	dissertation
d.	died
div.	division
ed.	edited, -or
encyc.	encyclopedia
et al.	and others (*et alii*)
et passim	here and there

e.g.	for example (*exempli gratia*)
et seq.	and the following (*et sequens*)
enl.	enlarged
ed. cit.	the edition cited
etc.	and so forth (*et cetera*)
ex.	example
esp.	especially
f.	following page
ff.	and the following pages
fig.	figure
fac.	facsimile
fasc.	fascicle
fl.	flourished, greatest development or influence
fn.	footnote
fol.	folio
front.	frontispiece
hist.	history, -ical, -ian
ibid.	in the same place (*ibidem*)
i.e.	that is (*id est*)
id. or idem.	that same work or page
infra.	below
illus.	illustrated, -tion
introd.	introduction, -ed
l.	line
loc. cit.	in the place cited (*loco citato*)
lang.	language
ms.	manuscript
n.n.	no name
n.d.	no date
n.b.	note well (*nota bene*)
numb.	numbered
n.s.	new series
n.p.	no place given for publication
no publ.	no publisher
op. cit.	in the work cited (*opere citato*)
O.S.	old series
par.	paragraph
pl.	plate
post	after

pub.	published, -ication
Ps.	Psalm
pt.	part
pseud.	pseudonym
pref.	preface
pp. 2ff.	page 2 and the following page
q.v.	which see, whom see (*quantum vis; quode vide*)
r. or recto	right-hand page of a book
rev.	revised
sec.	section
st.	stanza
sic	thus
ser.	series
sig.	signature
sc.	scene
scil.	to wit (*scilicet*)
supra	above
s.v.	under the word or heading (*sub verbo*)
trans.	translated, -or, -ion
v., vide	see
vol.	volume
v. or verso	left-hand page of a book
viz.	namely (*videlicet*)
v.s.	see above (*vide supra*)

How to Use This Sample Term Paper

As you will see, the numbers of the key ideas which appear in the text have been noted on the sample term paper. You may easily look up the explanation or the reason for the use of a particular form by turning back from the sample paper to the specific item in the text.

LINCOLN'S ASSASSINATION -- A MURDER MYSTERY

by

Gerald Driscoll

English 100A
Dr. David Archibald
May 1, 19--

LINCOLN'S ASSASSINATION -- A MURDER MYSTERY

The purpose of this paper is to point up some of the mysteries surrounding the tragic death of President Abraham Lincoln. The murder of this great man is considered to be one of the greatest tragedies befalling the American people. Another tragedy stemming from the murder is the apparent breakdown of jurisprudence and American justice which took place following the killing. With each passing year, the murder plot and subsequent assassination become more dimmed and the circumstances of the conspiracy, the act itself, and the trial are now hidden among a maze of abstractions and generalities with each writer's interpretation of the tragedy connected with the President. In fact, a perusal of any number of books on the subject reveals inconsistencies, gaps, confusions, and widely differing opinions on the events leading up to and following the killing. This term paper will include official government evidence and will attempt to present facts rather than fiction about Lincoln's murder.

It is common knowledge that John Wilkes Booth killed Lincoln, but the part played by those who went on trial for their lives as accomplices in the atrocious crime is still clouded in a veil of mystery.

(188)   (207)

This paper will pinpoint certain events connected
with the assassination -- events that to this day con-
tribute to the fact that President Lincoln's assassination
is indeed a murder mystery.

(210) Lincoln's premonition of death

The years have not unfolded the reason why Lincoln
acted so strangely on the day he was shot. He appeared
to be extremely melancholy and expressed the fear that
men were attempting to do him harm. In fact, when leaving
the White House for Ford's Theatre, he said "good-bye"
rather than his customary "good night" to his servant.
This attitude of impending disaster and other statements
made by Lincoln lead one to wonder from what source his
fears originated. He took a fatalistic view of a possible
assassination, however, when he said, "No use worrying.
What is to be, must be. If anyone is really determined to
kill me, I shall be killed!"[1]

Lack of adequate protection provided for the President

It would almost appear that Lincoln never had a
chance to escape from death the night of April 14. Four
instances will illustrate this. First, Mrs. Lincoln
dismissed the regular guard and had requested that the
President's life be protected by a metropolitan policeman by the name of Parker. It must be assumed that Mrs.
Lincoln did not know that Parker had a reputation for

(222)
(147)

[1] Richard N. Current, Mr. Lincoln (New York: Dodd,
Mead and Co., 1957), p. 382.

drunkenness while on duty, of conduct unbecoming an
officer, and of leaving his post without proper authority.[2]   In fact, protective measures to guard the life
of the President were criminally negligent. Second,
the armed guard Parker, whom Mrs. Lincoln had requested
and whose duty it was to stand outside the presidential
box and "screen" all passers-by, was mysteriously absent
from his post at the time Booth made his fateful entry.
Third, no one had bothered to notice the peephole in
the door that Booth had bored on the morning of the
murder. Four, the broken lock on the door of the presidential box had not been repaired. Into all these errors,
omissions, and faulty security measures did the President
of the United States walk.

(190)   On the night of April 14, 1865, he /Lincoln7 (75)
attended a performance of Our American Cousin at
Ford's Theatre in Washington. A few minutes
after 10 o'clock, a shot rang through the crowded
house. John Wilkes Booth, one of the best-known
actors of the day, had shot the President in the
head from the back of the Presidential box.[3]

This tragedy gave rise to even more tragedies and set
off one of the most mixed-up manhunts and criminal trials
ever to be conducted anywhere.

---

(149)   [2]Otto Eisenschiml, Why Was Lincoln Murdered? (New
York: Grosset and Dunlap, 1937), pp. 12, 14.

          [3]"Assassination," The World Book Encyclopedia (150)
(1950), 10:4472.

After shooting Lincoln,[4] Booth jumped from the presidential box onto the stage, catching his right spur in the U. S. Treasury flag. This unforeseen accident was to implicate and ruin the life of one Dr. Samuel Mudd, physician, who at this moment may very well have been completely unaware of Booth's intentions or activities.[5] We will speak more of Dr. Mudd later.

Booth's change of plans from kidnaping to murder

John Wilkes Booth was a nationally known actor and the grandson of a man who helped runaway slaves escape. John Wilkes was unlike his grandfather in that he (John) was a strong southern sympathizer. Kelly makes an interesting statement regarding Booth's motives in the crime when he says:

> Which of the shadows hid the demoniacal movements of the man who cast himself in the role of the villain in the arch tragedy of his own authorship that night, remains a mystery.[6]

(153)

Booth, the idol of the American stage, was a strange and vain man indeed. His income amounted to over $20,000 a year, and he had everything he could possibly want, except perhaps undying fame as the executioner of a "tyrant,"

---

(144)   [4]A single-shot, muzzle-loading, .41-caliber Derringer pistol was used.

[5]U. S. Dept. of the Interior, Lincoln Museum and the House Where Lincoln Died, Booklet, reprint (Washington, 1956), p. 14.

(157)   [6]Edward James Kelly, The Crime at Ford's Theatre (Washington: Government Service, Inc., Action Publishers, 1944), p. 4.

as he viewed Lincoln. Contrary to popular belief, he
originally had intended to kidnap the President and
exchange him for southern prisoners of war. The ex-
tent of southern losses, however, changed Booth's mind
about the practicability of such a move, and in its place
another plan had to be developed. The resulting trial
and historical accounts of the incident have never made
clear whether or not the persons convicted of the crime
of being accessories knew of Booth's change of plans from
kidnaping to murder.

Booth's decision to kill the President may have re-
sulted from Lincoln's statement of April 12,[7] that he
(Lincoln) hoped that the freed slaves of Louisiana would
be given the right to vote. Kelly remarked that when
Booth heard of this, he fumed loudly and said, "Now, by
God, I'll put him through!"[8] (156)

General Grant's strange behavior

Now let us consider General Grant for a moment.
The evening at Ford's Theatre was to honor Lincoln as
well as Grant and, unbeknown to either of them, both
men had been marked for murder by Booth. Lincoln had
asked the general and his wife to join the presidential
party. "Earlier in the morning, General and Mrs. Grant
had accepted an invitation from the President to accom-

---

(155) [7]During the closing days of the war in 1865.
(166) (164) [8]Kelly, loc. cit.

pany him and Mrs. Lincoln to the theatre."[9]

History has never satisfactorily explained why the general and his lady suddenly notified the President on the same afternoon of that terrible day that they would be unable to attend the performance. With this abrupt explanation, the Grants boarded the train and headed for New Jersey to visit their children who were attending a camp.[10] (117)

Lincoln invited several other people to attend in place of the Grants but all declined. Finally, the President was able to get a Miss Clara Harris, a daughter of a senator, and her escort, a Major Henry R. Rathbone, to join him in the presidential box. Does it not seem strange that the President of the United States had great difficulty in obtaining guests for the evening's performance of what was to be a gala affair?

Grant's behavior in his refusal to attend was indeed strange. Only sixteen months later during the presidency of Andrew Johnson, Grant accepted another invitation to attend a reception at the Executive Mansion because he considered such an invitation from the President to be tantamount to an order, and Grant had always prided himself by saying he never disobeyed an order. One must question why Grant did not consider Lincoln's

(159)   (160)

_____

[9]The Lincoln Museum, op. cit., p. 6.

(163) [10]Ibid.

invitation to be an order but did feel the need to obey the invitation of Johnson.

Stanton's famous last words about Lincoln

The dastardly deed had been done. Booth carried out his promise to "put him /Lincoln7 through," for on the morning of April 15, the President died. An untold number of accounts quote Stanton, Secretary of War, as saying, "Now he belongs to the ages" at the moment of Lincoln's death. Yet it is quite likely that this famous eulogy was never spoken by Stanton or by anyone else. Witnesses present at Lincoln's death later recount many versions of what Stanton was supposed to have said:

> Now he belongs to the angels
> Now he belongs to history
> And now he belongs to the ages
> Doctor, please lead in prayer /note the
> lack of any reference to the "ages" saying7
> Ah dear friend! there is none now to do me
> justice; none to tell the world of the
> anxious hours we have spent together!
> There lies the most perfect ruler of men the
> world has ever seen.[11]

Booth's escape into Maryland

And what of Booth all this time? He was suffering from the effects of a broken leg received in his fall to the stage. But let us retrace his steps.

Booth, considering himself to be a national hero now that he had rid the country of a "tyrant," made his escape from the theater by horseback and approached the

---

[11]Eisenschiml, op. cit., p. 482 ff.

sentry at the Navy Yard Bridge. From this point on,
history disagrees on what took place. One historical
account states that Booth passed himself off as a Maryland planter from "near Beantown."[12] The sentry, Sergeant
Silas T. Cobb, violated orders by allowing Booth to pass
through the gate after curfew. Eisenschiml's account of
the incident differs widely from Kelly's:

> A Sergeant Cobb, who was in charge at
> the north end of the bridge, had questioned
> Booth and, after a brief conversation, had
> let him pass. . . .   (72)

(74) . . . .

> It is characteristic of Booth that he
> did not hesitate to give his true name to the
> sentinel at the bridge, for, in the fantastic
> mind of the assassin, his act was to be the
> perfect crime of the ages, and he the most
> heroic assassin of all times![13]   (110)

. . . .

> To return to Sergeant Cobb, one can
> understand his decision to let Booth . . .
> pass unconditionally. . . . He /Cobb7 had to
> make his decisions, and he made them accord-
> ing to his best judgment. On what grounds can
> it be explained, however, that having heard
> Booth's name from his own lips, this soldier
> did not give the alarm as soon as the news of
> Lincoln's assassination reached him?[14]

Cobb's failure to mention Booth's passing through his
post was never brought up in the trial. Strange indeed that not one of the prosecuting officers asked
(199)

---

(194) [12]Kelly, op. cit., p. 15.

[13]Eisenschiml, op. cit., p. 107 f.

(166) [14]Ibid., pp. 108-09.

this guard why he, Cobb, never reported that Booth headed into Maryland.

Confusion rose to new heights in the hours immediately following Booth's cowardly shot. To cite one illustration, the New York _Herald_ carried news dispatches in every edition. In the rush to get out its first extra on the slaying, the _Herald_ misdated its paper by carrying the date Friday, April 14, on its masthead.[15]

Secretary of War Stanton's unexplained silence

A second strange event concerns the actions of the Secretary of War, Edwin Stanton. Rather than following the most logical course of action by releasing the name of the assassin to the newspapers as soon as possible as an aid in Booth's apprehension, Stanton withheld the name until several hours after the crime had been committed. A news dispatch of 1:30 a.m. appearing in the _Herald_ dated April 15 states "some evidence of the guilt of the (112) party who attacked the President is in the possession of the police."[16] (218)

The cloud of suspicion over Dr. Samuel Mudd

What was Booth doing during the hours immediately following the shooting? He had made a safe escape into Maryland although racked by pain from a broken leg bone. Because the home of Dr. Samuel Mudd, a general practitioner,

---

(158) [15]The true date was Saturday, April 15. New York _Herald_, Whole No. 10,456.

[16]The New York _Herald_, Saturday, April 15, 1865, p. 1, col. 4, lines 28-30.

was on Booth's escape route, it seems only natural that
Booth headed for the doctor's home to receive first aid.
Mudd may have been merely an unfortunate victim by his
apparent innocent acquaintanceship with Booth. The doctor received a life sentence for giving aid and comfort
to Booth. Several years after the trial, Mudd was par-
doned for his heroic medical deeds performed while he
served time in a federal prison. Mudd escaped the death
penalty because the court never proved that he was guilty
of being an accomplice in the crime. Consider the following facts in favor of the physician:

   a) He was a doctor sworn by oath to give aid to
      the injured.

   b) There is considerable doubt that Mudd knew of
      the shooting at Ford's Theatre when Booth
      approached him for treatment. Lack of rapid
      communication plus the fact that Mudd treated
      Booth only hours after the crime had been
      committed open serious doubts as to Mudd's
      knowledge of what Booth had done.

   c) Booth certainly did not intend to injure him-
      self at Ford's Theatre. He would have no
      reason, therefore, to include Dr. Mudd among
      his accomplices. Booth's arrival at Mudd's
      home for first aid may have been nothing more
      than a coincidence.

Mrs. Surrat's sacrifice

Booth and his confederates who actually wielded
pistol and dagger as they attacked government officials
marked for death along with Lincoln were obviously
guilty. Yet, history has not clearly established the
degree of guilt or innocence of any of the people who
went on trial and who in some cases forfeited their

freedom or their lives. For example, Dr. Mudd may have
been guilty only of knowing Booth. Mary Surrat may have
been found guilty because she had a son who was an active
southern courier and because she operated a boardinghouse
where Booth sometimes visited her son and other men found
guilty of the crime. "The trial of Mrs. Surrat, first
woman to be legally executed in the United States, pro-
voked unending controversy. Many held her to be innocent,
few believed her degree of guilt warranted hanging, but
the verdict remained unchanged."[17]

A case of mistaken identity

Perhaps the most intriguing and mystifying aspect
of the trial concerned the establishment of the identity of
John Wilkes Booth from a photograph. Witnesses to the
shooting were asked to identify the photograph as that
of the murderer -- John Wilkes Booth. This they failed
to do simply because all through the trial the photograph exhibited was that of John's brother Edwin, also
a famous actor and equally as well known as John.

> Yet, the photograph /of Edwin/ went un-
> noticed into the files of the trial and his-
> tory has failed to record this slip -- one of
> the most tragic mistakes in American juris-
> prudence.[18]

(114)

. . . .

Of all the mysteries and problems arising

_____

(211)   [17]Kelly, op. cit., p. 31.

[18]Eisenschiml, op. cit., pp. 264-65.

out of Lincoln's assassination, the enigma of
how Edwin's picture came to be substituted for
that of his brother John Wilkes is one of the
most intriguing.[19]

Booth's diary and the thirteen missing pages

Let us now turn our attention from the trial to the

diary kept by Booth. He had developed a habit of re-

cording interesting events of the day in a small blank

book.[20] After he was killed by federal troops (some

historians say he took his own life rather than be cap-

tured), the diary was discovered on his body and turned

over to the officer in charge. The diary eventually

found its way to the Secretary of War after having been

officially listed among the personal effects found on

Booth's body. Each of the pages in the diary was counted

and numbered. The officer called this to Stanton's atten-

tion when the diary was transferred to the Secretary's

care. However, when the diary was produced at the trial,

thirteen sequential pages in the middle of the book had

been torn out from the binding and were missing. The officer

in charge of the federal troops stated emphatically at the

court of investigation that the pages were all accounted

for when the diary was given to the Secretary. Stanton,

on the other hand, insisted that the pages were torn

from the diary before it was placed in his hands. It

---

[19]Ibid., p. 265.

[20]Frederick A. Morse, "The Trial of the Lincoln Assassins, A Probable Usurpation of Civil Justice." Unpublished
M.A. Thesis, The Graduate School of Cornell University, 1933,
pp. 65-66.

was a case of one man's word against another man's word.
Stanton, being the superior officer, convinced the court
that the pages were missing when he received the diary.

Why has this diary been referred to so many times
by historians? Of what importance was it? Why did the
colonel or Stanton lie about the missing pages? According to the colonel who claimed that he had read the
diary, the missing pages offered incriminating evidence
implicating men holding government office in Washington.
Although no office holder was mentioned by name, the iden-
tification of these individuals was eagerly sought after
by the investigating officers and the court of inquiry
but to no avail. Booth, the man who wrote the entries
in the diary, was shot and killed before he could be
questioned. Throughout the following years, historians
have searched diligently for clues leading to the identity
of the persons left nameless in Booth's diary.

Was Stanton implicated?

One name that keeps coming to the attention of
historians is that of Edwin M. Stanton, Secretary of War
during Lincoln's administration. It is the opinion of
Eisenschiml,[21] Bishop,[22] Sandburg,[23] and writers who

[21]Eisenschiml, op. cit., pp. 434-35.

[22]James Alonzo Bishop, The Day Lincoln Was Shot
(New York: Harper & Brothers, 1955), p. 257.

[23]Carl Sandburg, The Prairie Years and the War Years
(New York: Harcourt, Brace and Company, 1954), p. 723.

have documented the assassination that Stanton, a politically ambitious man and an outspoken critic of the President, acted in a very peculiar manner following the slaying. For example, why did he keep the name of the assassin a secret until three hours after the crime, knowing that every minute's delay reduced the chances for apprehending the criminal? No one has been able to explain Stanton's motives for withholding the name of the murderer when it was an established fact that the culprit was John Wilkes Booth.

Consider also how Stanton reacted to the news brought to him by the chief of detectives, General Lafayette G. Baker. Baker reported to Stanton, "We have got Booth." Stanton said nothing in return but waited a full minute in silence and then left the room without a word.[24] This was strange behavior for a man who should have been overjoyed at the news that the manhunt had been successful.

An interesting story of a coded message prepared by General Baker shortly before his death alleges that Stanton helped plot the murder of Lincoln.[25]

Time erases evidence

It is tragic that each passing year washes away

---

[24]Eisenschiml, op. cit., p. 150.

[25]Robert H. Fowler (ed), "Was Stanton Behind Lincoln's Murder?", Civil War Times, 3 (August-September 1961), 5.

another bit of evidence concerning the Lincoln murder.
Interpretations by different writers do not always agree.
In fact, the many different accounts serve to muddle the
affair even more than it already is. If one wishes to
judge Stanton on circumstantial evidence, then the finger
of suspicion points heavily at him. However, this is not
the American way to determine the guilt or innocence of
individuals.

Perhaps more would be known about the conspirators
in the killing of President Lincoln if the son of this
great man had not destroyed many of his father's personal
papers. In 1925, a year before his death, Robert Todd
Lincoln burned some of his father's unpublished papers.
He gave as his reason that he saw no useful way in which
the evidence contained in the letters and manuscripts
could be used. He further stated that the incident and
all connected with it were long since dead and he did not
wish to reopen the case. Robert Lincoln never elaborated
upon his comments and in so doing added more mysteries
to those that already surrounded the murder. We can only
conjecture as to the contents of the burned papers.[26]

It is almost a certainty that the motives for killing the President, the mysteries surrounding the event,
the identity of the conspirators, and the actions of individuals close to the President will never be fully known.

[26] Emanuel Hertz, The Hidden Lincoln (New York:
The Viking Press, 1938), Preface.

BIBLIOGRAPHY

(222) "Assassination," The World Book Encyclopedia (1950), 10:4472.

(195)

(223) Bishop, James Alonzo. The Day Lincoln Was Shot. New York: Harper & Brothers, 1955.

Current, Richard N. Mr. Lincoln. New York: Dodd, Mead and Co., 1957.

Eisenschiml, Otto. Why Was Lincoln Murdered? New York: Grossett and Dunlap, 1937.

(149) Fowler, Robert H. "Was Stanton Behind Lincoln's Murder?" Civil War Times, 3: 5-13, August-September, 1961.

Hertz, Emanuel. The Hidden Lincoln. New York: The Viking Press, 1938.

Kelly, Edward James. The Crime at Ford's Theatre. Washington: Government Service, Inc., Action Publishers, 1944.

Morse, Frederick A. "The Trial of the Lincoln Assassins, A Probable Usurpation of Civil Justice." Unpublished M.A. Thesis, The Graduate School of Cornell University, Ithaca, New York, 1933.

New York Herald, Saturday, April 15, 1865.

Sandburg, Carl. The Prairie Years and the War Years. New York: Harcourt, Brace and Company, 1954.

U. S. Department of the Interior. Lincoln Museum and the House Where Lincoln Died. Booklet, reprint. Washington: Government Printing Office, 1956.

INDEX